FRIENDS

OF ACPL

P9-DZA-302

When Snakes Attack!

Paul Hansen

Enslow Publishers, Inc.
40 Industrial Road
Box 398
Berkeley Heights, NJ 07922
USA

http://www.enslow.com

Copyright © 2006 by Enslow Publishers, Inc.

All rights reserved.

No part of this book may be reproduced by any means without the written permission of the publisher.

Library of Congress Cataloging-in-Publication Data

Hansen, Paul.
  When snakes attack! / by Paul Hansen.
     p. cm. — (When wild animals attack!)
  Includes bibliographical references and index.
  ISBN 0-7660-2667-1
  1. Snake attacks—Juvenile literature. I. Title. II. Series.
  QL666.O6H337 2006
  597.96—dc22

                                              2006017396

Printed in the United States of America

10 9 8 7 6 5 4 3 2 1

To Our Readers:
We have done our best to make sure all Internet Addresses in this book were active and appropriate when we went to press. However, the author and the publisher have no control over and assume no liability for the material available on those Internet sites or on other Web sites they may link to. Any comments or suggestions can be sent by e-mail to comments@enslow.com or to the address on the back cover.

Photo/Illustration Credits: Animals Animals - Earth Scenes/Degginger, E.R., pp. 3, 28; Animals Animals - Earth Scenes/Leszczynski, Zigmund, p. 39; Animals Animals - Earth Scenes/Schwartz, C.W., p. 16; Animals Animals - Earth Scenes/Whitehead, Fred, p. 26; Corel Stock Photos, pp. 3, 6, 17; Getty Images/AFP, p. 36; Getty Images/Aurora, p. 25; Getty Images/Discovery Channel Images, pp. 3, 22; Getty Images/National Geographic, pp. 12, 30; Getty Images/Stone, pp. 1, 3, 40; Courtesy of National Science Foundation, p. 11; Photo Researchers, Inc./Peter Chadwick, p. 21; Photo Researchers, Inc./Joseph T. Collins, p. 8; Photo Researchers, Inc./Suzanne L. & Joseph T. Collins, p. 9; Photo Researchers, Inc./Fletcher & Baylis, pp. 3, 34; Photo Researchers, Inc./Jim W. Grace, pp. 32–33; Photo Researchers, Inc./Jeffrey Lepore, p. 15; Photo Researchers, Inc./Tom McHugh, p. 14; Photos.com, p. 42; Visuals Unlimited/Jack Milchanowski, p. 4.

Illustration: Kevin Davidson, pp. 18–19

Cover Photos: Getty Images/Stone (front), Corel Stock Photos (back)

Contents

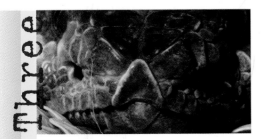

The pygmy rattlesnake is one of the smallest species of rattlesnakes. It is rarely more than two feet in length.

...gs of a coral snake (above)
...of the nonvenomous scarlet

...the House!

...snake found in North
..., which belongs to a
...ds. An elapid has short
...jaw, unlike a pit viper,
...ear-old Elaina Sawyer
...countered one in her
...lack, yellow, and red-
...kingsnake. She knew
...gerous, so she decided

Double Trouble!

It started out like a normal Sunday for James Cave of Oklahoma City, Oklahoma. After a hard week of work, it was time to do some chores. He was looking forward to working in his garden. He had no way of knowing that this autumn Sunday was going to be one he would never forget.

Cave kept all of his gardening tools along one wall of his garage. It would be one quick stop to get his shovel and rake before heading off to the garden. He never thought to look down and around the brush outside his home. It never occurred to him that he could be in danger in his own backyard.

Suddenly, Cave felt a sharp pain in his left foot. As he reached down to grab his throbbing foot, a gray snake with black and orange spots came out of the grass and bit his hand.

Shocked and surprised, Cave reeled up and fell backward over a barrel. He crashed to the ground. Right in front of him was another snake! This snake was larger than the first. It was light brown with darker brown markings. Before Cave could think or do anything, the second snake bit him in the right foot and then again in the groin.

Helpless and terrified, Cave called out to his wife and son. Within a short time, he vomited and shook all over. He could hardly breathe because his mouth had swollen so much. In a matter of moments, Cave had received four snakebites from two different kinds of venomous snakes, an extremely rare occurrence. Venomous snakes produce a poisonous fluid, which they use to defend themselves or to kill prey. The snakes' venom had poisoned James Cave.

)Snake)
FACT

Why Snakes Attack

Some snakes appear to be aggressive (likely to attack) during mating season, perhaps because they are trying to attract a mate. They are also known to be aggressive when they are cornered and have no way to escape. Some herpetologists (scientists that study snakes and other reptiles) believe that a snake will be aggressive toward a human if it perceives that its home territory is threatened. Other experts say that snakes are like people—some are just more aggressive than others. However, most experts agree that snakes are more likely to flee than attack a human.

The black, yellow, and red markin
can easily be confused with those
kingsnake (opposite).

A Coral Snake i

The other type of venomou
America is the coral snak
family of snakes called elapi
fangs at the front of its uppe
which has long fangs. Ten-y
from Wickham, Florida, en
home. Elaina thought the b
striped snake was a scarlet
that kingsnakes were not dan

to try to capture it. Big mistake! The snake was a deadly coral snake and it bit Elaina's right hand.

The girl's mother immediately called 911. A helicopter came to fly Elaina to the hospital, where she was treated with antivenin. Her heart was beating much too fast, and unevenly, at first. The doctors worried that she might not survive.

But Elaina was fortunate. She was treated quickly and survived. If a bite from a coral snake is not treated, the victim can become temporarily paralyzed (unable to move) or even die.

Venomous or not? This scarlet kingsnake is nonvenomous. Its markings are very similar to those of the venomous coral snake, however.

Coral snakes are rarely seen in cities, much less inside houses. Like James Cave's, Elaina Sawyer's snake encounter was highly unusual. Most of the thousands of species, or kinds, of snakes are not venomous, and they rarely attack. Snakes live almost everywhere on Earth—in deserts, forests, streams, and lakes. Some live in trees, some live underground, and some spend most of their time in water. Some snakes even live in the ocean. These

Dangerous Snakes

Most snakes pose no threat to humans, but about 20 percent of all snakes are venomous. Of these, the most dangerous can kill in a few moments. They include the:

death adder: Its venom is so powerful and moves through the body so fast that victims often die before they can be treated. The death adder is found in New Guinea and Australia.

fierce snake: This Australian snake has the most toxic, or poisonous, venom of any snake in the world.

Malayan krait: Half of all people bitten by this snake die, even with antivenin treatment. It is found in Southeast Asia.

saw scaled viper: This viper kills more people in Africa than all other snakes combined. It gets its name from rubbing the sides of its body together, which makes a rasping sound.

3 1833 05172 1634

The yellow-lipped sea krait lives in the warm waters of the Pacific Ocean. Unlike other sea snakes, it must return to land to lay its eggs.

sea snakes are venomous and can be deadly. They can be found in the warm waters of the Pacific and Indian Oceans.

Only a few areas of the world have no snakes at all. In these areas, such as the polar regions and on the highest mountains, the ground stays frozen all year round. Snakes cannot survive in such cold places.

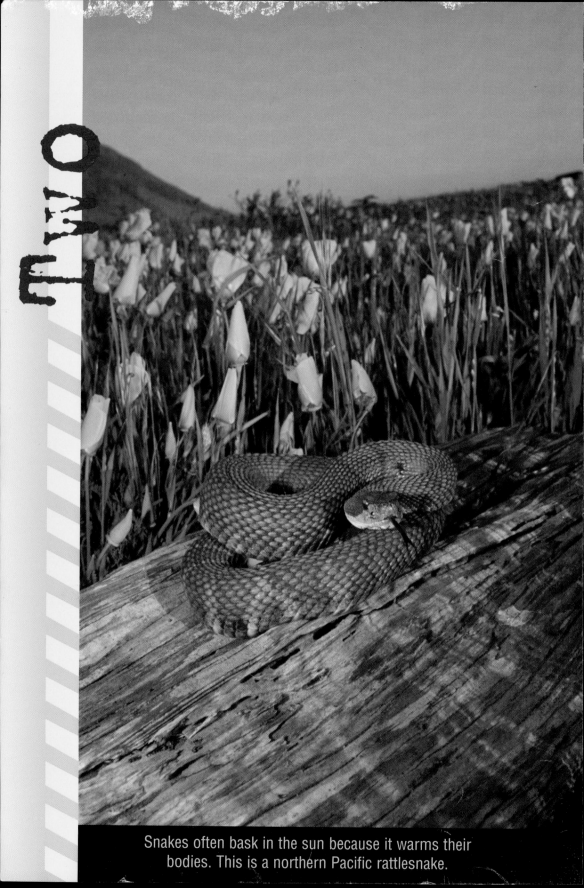

TWO

Snakes often bask in the sun because it warms their
bodies. This is a northern Pacific rattlesnake.

All About Snakes

There are about 2,700 species of snakes in the world. Snakes are reptiles, like lizards, turtles, alligators, and crocodiles. Most reptiles have scaly skin and are ectothermic, which means they do not produce enough heat by themselves to warm their bodies. They must adjust their body temperature by moving to warmer or cooler spots. For this reason, snakes can often be found warming themselves in the sun or going underground or in the shade to cool off if they get too hot.

Most snakes live in warm, tropical climates. Those that live in colder climates hibernate, or stay in a sleeplike state, in the winter because the temperature is too low for them to stay active. They find caves or underground dens, where the temperature is warmer, to escape the cold winter. Sometimes hundreds of snakes hibernate in the same den.

Snakes come in many sizes. Most adult snakes are between two and four feet long. The smallest snake in the world is the dwarf blind snake, found only on a few islands in the

Caribbean. It is about four inches long and feeds on tiny prey like insects and worms. The longest snake in the world is the reticulated python. These pythons can reach a length of thirty-five feet!

All snakes have camouflage, meaning that they blend in with their surroundings. This helps protect them from predators. Snakes come in a variety of colors and patterns, including black, green, and gray with brown diamonds. Different types of snakes are colored to help them survive in their own habitats.

All snakes also have scales, which are made of material similar to human fingernails. Under the

Not all snakes hibernate. Those that do, like these rattlesnakes, spend the winter in caves or underground dens.

An eastern garter snake molts, or sheds its skin. The clear scales that covered the snake's eyes can be seen in the molted skin.

scales is a layer of skin. As the outer scales wear down, new layers of skin and scales are produced from inside. Once they are fully formed, the old skin and scales come off. This happens throughout a snake's life. A snake helps this process, called molting, by rubbing its nose on something rough, and then crawling right out of its skin. Molting may take from two weeks to three months.

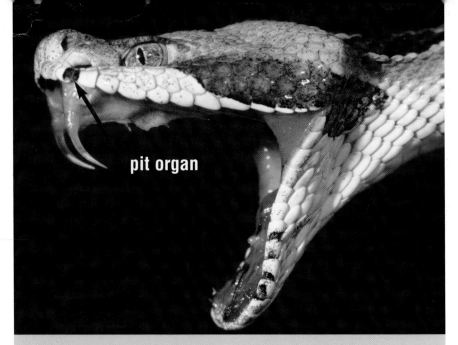

pit organ

A pit viper's heat-sensing pit organs are located in front of its eyes. Its fangs are hollow for injecting venom.

Venomous Snakes

Of the 20 percent of snake species that are venomous, many cannot hurt humans because they are too small or have rear fangs. Snakes with rear fangs are not as dangerous because they inject venom only after the prey has been partially eaten.

Even so, that leaves about two hundred types of venomous snakes that can attack humans. Venomous snakes have many of the same characteristics as nonvenomous snakes, plus other special features that help them survive.

For example, pit vipers have two special organs that sense heat. These pit organs are located on the snake's head. Using them, a pit viper can locate another animal by sensing the heat it

Snake Senses

A snake's eyes are located on either side of its head. This gives it a wide field of view. Instead of eyelids, snakes have clear scales over their eyes, which are replaced each time they molt. They can see and feel movement well, but most snakes cannot focus beyond a short distance.

A snake's ears are not visible on the outside of its body. Instead, snakes have inner ears. They pick up sound vibrations in their jawbones from the ground or other solid objects. These "sound" messages are sent to the inner ear,

allowing the snake to hear the sounds. Snakes cannot hear sounds through the air, like humans can.

A snake does not smell with a nose. Instead, a snake uses its long, forked tongue to smell. The tongue picks up tiny particles of scent from the air, the ground, and other objects. When the snake pulls its tongue back into its mouth, these particles enter the Jacobson's organ, two hollow sacs in the roof of the snake's mouth. The organ recognizes the smell and sends a message to the brain that tells if it is a mate, an enemy, or something good to eat.

Western Diamondback Rattlesnake FACTs

Length: Up to four feet on average, but can grow to more than seven feet

Weight: From four to ten pounds. The average weight is five pounds.

Diet: Small mammals such as prairie dogs, rabbits, gophers, chipmunks, ground squirrels, mice, and rats

Habitat: From desert flats to rocky hillsides, and grassy plains, forested areas, river bottoms, and coastal prairies

Life span: 25 years on average, although some have lived as long as 30 years

gives off. Even in complete darkness, a pit viper can detect and strike its prey.

Most venomous snakes that are dangerous to humans have hollow front fangs. When a venomous snake bites, it injects venom through the fangs into its victim. The venom is made in the venom glands on each side of the upper jaw.

Pit vipers have long, moveable fangs. When the snake is not attacking prey, these fangs are folded up along the roof of the mouth. When a pit viper strikes, the fangs come down and lock into place.

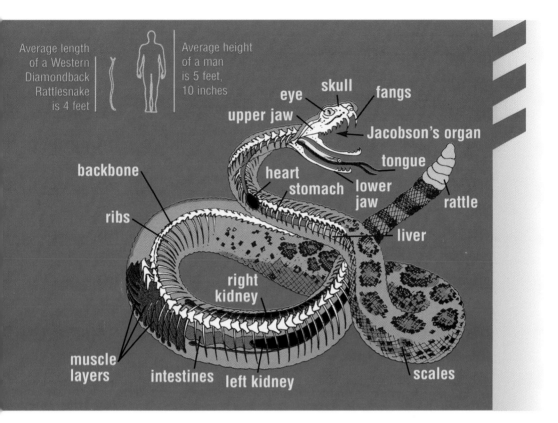

Average length of a Western Diamondback Rattlesnake is 4 feet

Average height of a man is 5 feet, 10 inches

How Snakes Eat

All snakes are carnivores. This means they eat other animals for food. Depending on their size and where they live, snakes eat eggs, fish, lizards, birds, rabbits, and small rodents such as mice, squirrels, and rats. Large snakes can eat small wild pigs, crocodiles, and even deer with antlers!

While hunting, some snakes stay in one place and wait for their prey to come near. Others may follow the scent trail of an animal. Many snakes hunt in water and use their speed to capture their prey—in fact, many snakes are faster in water than on land.

Snakes eat their prey whole. Most snakes can eat animals bigger than their heads because of the way their jaws are designed. The top and bottom jaws are not connected by bone, so the mouth can open extra wide. In addition, the two bones of the bottom jaw are separate so they can also move apart. A snake's skeleton is flexible enough to allow its ribs to separate, and the muscles and other material that connect the bones are very stretchy and flexible. This allows some snakes to eat animals much larger than their heads. Other snakes, however, such as coral snakes, have very small heads and cannot eat larger animals.

Largest and Smallest

The largest venomous snake in the world is the king cobra. Found in India, southern China, and throughout Southeast Asia, it can grow to be almost twenty feet long. Its venom is so strong that a full-grown elephant will die if bitten by a king cobra.

The smallest venomous snake in the world is the crowned black-headed snake. Rarely longer than ten inches, it is found in the southwestern United States. It feeds on centipedes and other small insects. Because the snake is so small, it cannot produce enough venom to injure a human.

An African rock python eats a young impala (a deer-like animal). The prey is eaten headfirst so the legs fold along its body.

A snake usually eats its prey headfirst. That way, the prey's legs fold along its body and it more easily moves through the snake's digestive tract. Strong muscles start pushing it toward the snake's stomach. Even when a snake's throat is stuffed with an animal two or three times bigger than its head, it can still breathe through a windpipe that extends to the front of its mouth.

After eating, a snake rests while its food digests. Depending on the size of the meal, this can go on for several weeks or months!

Three

A rattlesnake's distinctive rattle is sometimes heard just before it strikes. It can serve as an effective warning to predators.

Rattler Attack!

Ann Avery of Golden, Colorado, was out for an afternoon walk with her husband, Bill, in the beautiful open foothills that surround their home. Suddenly, it felt as if something small and bony hit her very hard on the ankle.

Ann looked down and, horrified, realized that she had been bitten by a rattlesnake. She had not seen or heard it before it struck.

She screamed, jumped over a bush, and started running down the trail. Her husband caught up with her and told her to try to stay calm while he went to get the car. The pain was already shooting up her leg as she waited.

Soon, Ann and Bill were speeding to the hospital. In the fifteen minutes it took to get there, Ann went temporarily blind. Her mouth was numb and her throat was swollen. She was having trouble breathing and her blood pressure dropped dangerously low. There was massive swelling around the wound on her ankle, and the flesh there was turning black and blue.

A Dangerous Dance

A snake dance is a sacred ceremony of the Hopi Indians of northeastern Arizona. The ceremony is held each August and lasts nine days. During the first four days, the men of a Hopi group called the Snake Society hunt rattlesnakes on their reservation, or homeland. Later in the ceremony, the men, who are experts at handling rattlesnakes, dance with the live snakes in their mouths! After the dance, they release the snakes back into the wild.

The Hopi believe that snakes can bring good luck. Through these ceremonies, the Hopi call on supernatural powers for rain, good harvests, and good health. The Hopi have been performing these ceremonies for many, many years. Nevertheless, it is very dangerous to pick up a venomous snake for any reason, and no one should attempt it.

The doctor who treated Ann said that if they had arrived at the hospital five minutes later, she might have died. Ann's severe reaction may have been the result of the snake's fangs hitting a vein, which sent the venom quickly through her bloodstream. Ann spent five days in the hospital before returning home.

Rattlesnakes are a type of pit viper and live in southern Canada, in almost every state in the United States, and throughout Central and South America. They are named for the distinctive rattle at the end of their tails. The rattle is created through the frequent molting of the snake's skin. With each molt, a new segment appears on the rattle. The purpose of the rattle is to startle predators. It acts as a warning to larger animals or humans that threaten the snake.

The main purpose of a rattlesnake's—or any snake's—venom is to help it get food. There are two types of poisons in snake venom that help kill prey. The first, neurotoxins, attack the nervous system of the prey and cause its throat to swell so that it is almost impossible to breathe. Neurotoxins also make the heart beat irregularly.

The rattle on the end of a rattlesnake's tail is formed through the process of molting.

Rattler in the Water

On a hot summer day, Kevin Edwards and his friend Ryan DeChamp decided to go swimming in the Consumnes River in Sacramento County, California. Edwards had almost stepped on a rattlesnake the week before while walking along the shore, so he was careful to watch where he stepped.

But he did not know that rattlesnakes are excellent swimmers. Edwards swam underwater for a few strokes. When he came up to the surface there was a rattlesnake staring him right in the eye! Before Edwards could do anything, the snake

bit him on the neck. Then it started swimming toward his friend. Edwards yelled out a warning and DeChamp was able to get away from the three-foot-long rattlesnake.

The two friends quickly made it to shore and called 911. Within minutes, Edwards was taken by helicopter to the hospital. During the eight-minute flight he felt a tingly sensation all over, and was very dizzy. His mouth had swollen shut and he had trouble swallowing. He spent four days in the hospital and received sixteen vials of antivenin.

The second type of poisons, hemotoxins, damage the prey's blood vessels and body tissues such as skin and muscles. Hemotoxins cause the area around the bite to swell and turn colors such as black, blue, green, and purple. Most snakes have one type of poison or the other. A very dangerous few have both.

Types of Rattlesnakes

There are approximately thirty-five species of rattlesnakes in the United States. They include the:

eastern diamondback: This is the largest snake in North America. It can grow to be eight feet long, but the average length is five feet. Found in the Southeast, it is named for the dark diamond shapes on its back, outlined with yellowish borders.

western diamondback: This snake grows to an average length of four feet. Western diamondbacks live in the Southwest and in northern Mexico. They are marked with dark diamond shapes outlined in white.

pygmy rattlesnake: One of the smallest species of rattlesnakes, it is usually less than two feet long. It lives in the Midwest and Southeast and is grayish-brown with rounded darker gray markings along the center of its back.

Four

The coral snake is in the elapid family of snakes. Other elapid species include cobras, mambas, and kraits.

Coral Snakes

Humans are not the only ones affected by venomous snakebites. One early fall afternoon, a seven-year-old golden retriever named Brutus was bitten by a coral snake while protecting his family. Brutus attacked and killed the snake after he spotted it moving close to the family as they were picnicking on the grass, but not before it bit him in the leg.

Brutus was taken to an animal emergency hospital and given antivenin. He recovered, but walked with a limp afterward. For his efforts, he won the National Hero Dog Award, given to family pets that perform acts of bravery that save the lives of family members. Brutus's thankful family recognizes that the old saying about a dog being man's best friend is certainly true.

Another dog was not as fortunate. Backdraft was a one-year-old Dalmatian owned by firefighter Richard Miller of Port St. Lucie, Florida. One evening, Backdraft came in from outside and seemed playful for a moment. But soon he

Cobras, like coral snakes, are members of the elapid family. This is a black forest cobra, found in Africa.

dropped to the floor. His breathing became shallow, he started to vomit, and he could not lift his head.

Backdraft was rushed to an emergency veterinary hospital where blood tests confirmed that he had been bitten by a coral snake. Miller began a desperate search for antivenin.

The fire rescue department in Miami-Dade County, Florida, had some on hand and was willing to donate it to the dog. But how would they get it to Port St. Lucie, two hours away by car? They were unable to find an airplane. Miller was about to make the drive to Miami to get the antivenin when word came that a helicopter pilot had volunteered to make the flight.

The antivenin was given to Backdraft and he fought bravely for hours, but finally died from the poisons. "He was part of the family," said Miller. Still a young dog, Backdraft was not able to fight off the effects of the very toxic venom of this snake.

The dog was rushed to an emergency veterinary hospital. He had been bitten by a coral snake.

Coral snakes, which belong to the elapid family of snakes, are found in the southeastern United States, and live in forests, along rivers and ditches, and in grasslands. While the coral snake is the only elapid to live in North and South America, there are many species of elapids in Australia. Cobras, from Africa and Asia, are also members of the elapid family.

Unlike those of pit vipers, the fangs of coral snakes and other elapids are short and do not move, but are fixed in place. Another difference between coral snakes and pit vipers is

How Snakes Move

Although snakes are legless, they are able to move about with ease. A snake's backbone allows it to bend and flex easily. Snakes have four main ways of moving:

rectilinear locomotion: This method is used to climb trees and "crawl" rather than slither on flat ground. The snake keeps its body straight and uses its muscles to pull its belly forward. It then pushes its scales down and backward and moves forward like a caterpillar.

undulation: The snake uses its body to form a series of flowing S shapes to move along the ground.

concertina: The snake moves the front of its body forward and then folds it into a zigzag shape. Then the snake pulls its back end forward and folds it into a zigzag. This process is repeated again and again. This style is named after a type of old-fashioned accordion.

sidewinding: This is used by snakes to move across sand. The snake lifts the front of its body and moves it sideways into an arch. Then the front end stops and the back end is lifted and moved sideways.

that coral snakes have small heads, the same size as their bodies. Because of this, coral snakes cannot swallow animals larger than their heads, and feed mainly on other snakes and lizards.

Coral snakes are brightly colored with red, yellow, and black stripes, and adults are usually between two and four feet in length. A coral snake's markings can easily be mistaken for those of certain nonvenomous snakes, such as the scarlet kingsnake or milk snake. This is one reason that coral snakes are considered very dangerous.

A rhyme about the order of the colored stripes can help distinguish the venomous coral snake from a nonvenomous snake: "Red and yellow kills a fellow. Red and black is safe for Jack."

Five

A reticulated python wraps itself around a
tree in Malaysia in Southeast Asia.

Snakes That Squeeze

A terrible and extremely rare attack happened in a small town in South Africa in the spring of 2002. A ten-year-old boy was eaten by a twenty-foot-long African rock python. The attack was made even worse by the fact that several other boys hid in nearby mango trees and watched in horror as the snake ate their friend. They were afraid to move and too terrified to try to rescue him.

Later, one of the boys, eleven-year-old Khaye Buthelezi, took the local police to where the attack occurred and told them what happened. "The snake quickly wrapped itself around [the boy's] body, pinning his arms to his side. He didn't scream, and neither did the rest of us—we didn't want the snake to come and take us as well," Khaye said.

The snake had squeezed and squeezed until the young boy died. Over the next three hours, the snake slowly swallowed the boy. Finally, the snake moved away and the other boys came down from the trees.

This is the only known instance in history in which a snake has eaten a human being. Most snakes are threatened by humans and try to avoid them. Even giant snakes such as pythons, anacondas, and boas usually stay away from people. These very large snakes belong to a group known as constrictors.

Constrictors live near water and are found only in tropical areas of South America, Africa, and Asia. None of them exist in the wild in North America, although many zoos around the United States keep these snakes in their herpetology centers, which are places where snakes and other reptiles are studied.

Herpetologists say that the South African python that killed the boy had probably just

Zoo workers in Germany handle an anaconda. It is eleven and a half feet long and weighs more than eighty-eight pounds.

awakened from its winter hibernation and was extremely hungry. Craig Smith, a snake expert who lives in the area, was amazed that a python would eat a human.

The boys of that South African village will never forget what happened that day. It was a rare and horrible experience.

Constrictors

Pythons, anacondas, and boas are among the largest living reptiles on Earth, growing up to thirty-five feet long. Like all snakes, they are carnivores. But instead of poisoning their prey, these snakes kill their prey by constriction. This means they coil their bodies around their victims and squeeze them until they suffocate (die from lack of air). Then they slowly swallow their victims whole. Pythons usually bite their prey to hold and immobilize, or stop, it before wrapping themselves tightly around the prey to kill it.

Anacondas are the heaviest snakes in the world. They can weigh up to six hundred pounds (about the same as three large men) and have bodies that measure one foot in diameter.

Pythons and anacondas look similar, but there are some important differences. Pythons have teeth on the front bone of the upper jaw. Anacondas do not. The biggest difference is that a python lays eggs while an anaconda's young are born live. In fact, one anaconda can give birth to over fifty baby snakes, each more than three feet long! Young constrictors have many predators. When they are small, the same animals that a large constrictor might eat might eat

Snakes That Make Good Pets

Having a pet snake is a big responsibility. Most snakes can live for about twenty years! That means a pet snake will require a lot of care and attention for a long time. If you are thinking about adopting a pet snake, also keep these points in mind:

Snakes should never be taken from the wild and kept as pets. Not only can this be dangerous for both you and the snake, it is against the law. Only a few kinds of snakes make good pets. Smaller snakes such as corn snakes and garter snakes are two of these. No venomous snakes and only certain constrictors (such as corn snakes) are recommended as pets. Any good shop that specializes in reptiles will carry the snake species that make the best pets.

You will need special equipment to care for your snake, including a home called a vivarium for the snake to live in. The vivarium should be a box at least twice as long as the snake. It should have a heater and a bowl with clean water. It also needs special lighting or needs to be near a window to keep the snake warm.

Snakes are very good at escaping, so you will need to keep track of your snake at all times. It should be kept in a secure area whenever you are not directly watching it.

An African rock python has killed its prey, a white rat, by constricting (squeezing) it. Now it begins its meal.

them. For example, a wild pig might eat a young boa one day and be eaten itself by a full-grown boa the next day.

Humans are constrictors' greatest enemy. Unfortunately, some people like to have the skin of a boa or python for a trophy, and so these snakes are hunted by bounty hunters. Although bounty hunting is illegal around the world, criminals still do it for the money they receive from irresponsible dealers.

Meanwhile, as rain forests are being destroyed by humans, so is the habitat of these large and powerful snakes. Many herpetologists feel that most large snakes will become extinct, or disappear from Earth, in the not too distant future if nothing is done to protect them.

six

Western diamondback rattlesnakes are found in the southwestern United States and northern Mexico.

When a Snake Bites

Venomous snakes live in nearly every state in the United States. They generally live in areas that are far away from humans. But as people build more and more homes in areas that used to be wild, they come into contact with snakes more often. Most snake attacks are provoked, which means they happen when a human has surprised a snake (even if they did not do so intentionally) or has tried to pick up or handle a snake.

There are many precautions you can take to avoid being bitten by a venomous snake if you spend time in snake country. Before you set out, have a short meeting with your group to go over a simple emergency plan that includes knowing your route and destination. How far will you be from a town or medical center? Will you be able to get cell phone reception? Know how to contact a ranger if you are in a park. Plan to hike as a group. If someone in the group gets bitten, others can go for help or assist in getting the victim out of the area.

Many snakes live near water, so be especially careful around lakes, rivers, and streams. When hiking, wear long pants and boots to protect your feet and ankles.

Walk on clear paths and carry a walking stick. Snakes generally avoid human pathways and are much more visible if they should happen onto a clear path. A walking stick can keep a snake at a safe distance and also be effective at scaring the snake away from you and your group.

Never reach into an area such as a hole or cave without first looking into it. If you do see a snake, quickly move away. Watch for other snakes in the same area.

What to Do in Case of a Bite

The signs of a bite vary with the type of snake. A bite from a pit viper, including a rattlesnake, looks like a puncture mark.

Experts agree that wearing long pants and boots while hiking is one of the best ways to avoid being bitten by a venomous snake in case of an accidental encounter.

It produces immediate pain. Symptoms from a coral snake bite, on the other hand, may not appear until up to twelve hours after the bite. The bite appears like tiny scratches in a semicircle.

The most important thing to do in case of a snakebite is to get to a medical center as soon as possible. A lot has been learned about how to treat snakebites, but the most important factor is time.

The most important thing to do in case of a snakebite is to get to a medical center as soon as possible.

This is especially true for young people. Poison works faster in a smaller body simply because it does not have to go as far before it reaches a major organ. Most experts agree that a snakebite should be treated within four hours. Each case is different since the type of snake, the amount of venom injected, and the size of the victim must be considered.

However, there are times when a snakebite occurs a long distance from any hospital. In these cases it is best to keep the victim quiet and calm. Movement of the body will make the heart beat faster. A faster heart rate can move the venom through the body quicker.

If an arm or leg is bitten, remove any clothing and jewelry and put the arm or leg in a position level with or below the heart. This will slow the movement of the venom.

If a victim is not able to reach medical care within thirty minutes, the American Red Cross recommends that a bandage be applied, wrapped two to four inches above the bite to help slow the venom reaching the heart and causing the poison to spread throughout the body. It should be loose enough to slip a finger underneath.

Snake Questions

Can snakes swim? Yes, most can. Snakes that live in water move by forming their bodies into s-shaped curves. The rear edge of each curve pushes against the water to send the snake on its way.

Can snakes jump? Most snakes can jump or strike about the length of their bodies. The African carpet viper can coil its body like a spring and then shoot straight up about three feet.

Can snakes fly? No, not even the so-called flying snakes of Southeast Asia. These snakes actually glide through the air and can go more than eighty feet! They hurl themselves into the air from a tall tree toward the branches of a lower tree. As they do, they raise their ribs and flatten their bodies to form a parachute.

When Snakes Attack!

Most venomous snakebites are treated with antivenin. Most hospitals have at least some antivenin available for snakebites. A doctor injects the antivenin into the victim through the veins or muscle tissues. This can stop the effects of the snake venom.

For many years, some experts believed that it was a good idea to try and suck out the venom from the snakebite. But today many experts feel that this is not a good idea. They suggest washing the wound out if there is water available. Otherwise, keeping the victim calm and as comfortable as possible is the best advice.

It is not necessary to fear snakes more than any other creature. Certainly venomous snakes are dangerous, but they generally avoid humans. There are many more dangerous creatures on the planet, both wild and domestic. In fact, dogs bite millions of Americans each year, and almost 800,000 bites— one out of every six—are serious enough to require medical attention. On the other hand, between ten and twelve people die from snakebites each year in the United States. This includes those who keep venomous snakes as pets, against the advice of snake experts.

The more we understand the habits of the many different kinds of snakes in our world, the better we will be able to appreciate and protect these creatures.

Glossary

antivenin—A substance that can stop the effects of a venomous snakebite.

carnivore—An animal that eats only meat.

den—A cave or other place where a snake makes its home or hibernates.

ectothermic—Unable to regulate body temperature. An ectothermic animal's body temperature is determined and is affected by its surroundings.

habitat—The area in which an animal lives. A suitable habitat includes enough water, food, space, and shelter.

herpetologist—A scientist who studies reptiles and amphibians.

hibernate—To go into a long-term, deep sleep during which an animal's heart rate and breathing slow down to conserve energy.

molt—To shed skin.

predator—An animal that hunts and eats other animals.

prey—An animal that is hunted and eaten by another animal.

species—A group of plants or animals that have similar characteristics and can produce young.

venom—A fluid injected by a bite, used to stop prey or for defense. Once injected, it is toxic, or poisonous.

venomous—Producing a poisonous fluid and capable of inflicting a poisonous bite or sting.

Books

Gibbons, Whit. *Snakes of the Southeast*. Atlanta: University of Georgia Press, 2005.

O'Shea, Mark. *Venomous Snakes of the World*. Princeton, N.J.: Princeton University Press, 2005.

Ricciuti, Ed. *The Snake Almanac*. Guilford, Conn.: Lyons Press, 2001.

Ruth, Maria Mudd. *Snakes*. Tarrytown, N.Y.: Benchmark Books, 2002.

Zug, George R. and Carl H. Ernst. *Smithsonian Answer Book: Snakes*. Washington, D.C.: Smithsonian Books, 2004.

Internet Addresses

Discovery Channel: Snakes
<http://www.exn.ca/snakes/>

PBS Nature: Victims of Venom
<http://www.pbs.org/wnet/nature/victims/>

Pet Reptile Information
<http://www.petreptiles.com/index.php3>

Index